LUIS SECO DE LUCENA PAREDES

LA ALHAMBRA
DE
GRANADA

Fotografías:

Oronoz - J. Ciganovic - J. Padial Peramos
Miguel Sánchez - Edistudio - Catalá Roca - Salmer

EDITORIAL EVEREST, S. A.

MADRID • LEON • BARCELONA • SEVILLA • GRANADA • VALENCIA
ZARAGOZA • BILBAO • LAS PALMAS DE GRAN CANARIA • LA CORUÑA
PALMA DE MALLORCA • ALICANTE — MEXICO • BUENOS AIRES

SEPTIMA EDICION

© by EDITORIAL EVEREST, S. A.
Carretera León-Coruña, km 5 - LEÓN (Spain)
ISBN-84-241-4709-X
Legal deposit: LE-591-1984
Printed in Spain

EDITORIAL EVERGRAFICAS, S. A. - Carretera León-La Coruña, km 5 - LEON (España)

THE ALHAMBRA OF GRANADA

Usually you go up to the *Alhambra* by the *Cuesta de los Gomérez*, which starts at *Plaza Nueva* and ends at the *Puerta de las Granadas*, built by the Christians during Charles V's period in that stretch of the walls that ran from *Torres Bermejas*, at the top of the *Mawrūr* Hill, to *Bāb al-Difāf* or the *Puerta de los Tableros*. Its rests are known today as *Cadi* Bridge that crosses the *Darro* River. At this same place, there was a fortified tower that defended *Bāb al-Jandaq* or the *Puerta del Barranco*, named by the Arabs after the geographic site where it was located. This gate was one of the entrances to the *medina* or city of Granada.

Once the *Puerta de las Granadas* is passed, we go inside the *Sabīka* Precipice or «melted silver» precipice, transformed today into a luxuriant forest, through which three foot-paths climb. The one at the left leads us to the *Puerta de la Explanada*, which the people call of the Justice, the most important entrance to the *Alhambra*. Before reaching this gate, and next to a small tower that defends it, we find the beautiful Charles V's Pillar. The Count of

1. —*Door of the Pomegranates*

2. —*The Alhambra Woods*

3. *Charles V pillar*

Tendilla ordered to build it, and it was constructed by Nicolao de Corte, according to Machuca's sketches. It is formed by two bodies, which rise on top of the column. The first of the two is decorated with beautiful figure-heads. The second one carries an inscription, surmounted by the Emperor's sculptured code of arms enclosed in a semicircle.

The central path of the forest, which widens itself into three squares along its way, leads to the *Generalife*. On the second square, ornamented by a fountain, as in the third one, rises a monument, which the city built to honor the memory of its illustrious son, the famous essay writer Angel Ganivet. Finally, the path to the right carries us close to *Torres Bermejas*, and to the famous Camp of the Martyrs, where the Christians suffered captivity inside the dungeons.

This forest, covered by many different species of plants, being the black poplar the most frequent; where the sunrays are filtered through the branches of exhuberant trees, separating themselves in gentle tones; in which all kinds of birds nest, particularly blackbirds and nightingales, and in which tiny streams run through its avenues where, as the poet said, «the water cries, grieves, sighs, sings and laughs», and where falls run «like a torrent echo», offers the visitor, during the hot summer months, an easy, fresh and calm retirement, that invites to meditation and to a quiet and nice rest.

* * *

Let us go inside and visit the *Alhambra*. It will surprise us the strong contrast of its architecture. The fortifications are remarkable: solid and high fortified towers of amazing structure, rising at the edge of precipices and steep cliffs, which make them inaccessible; with no more openings in their façades than loopholes; massive and huge walls, built with very hard rocks, protected by wide ramparts, interior pit and part of the wall in the most dangerous zones; difficult entrances defended by double gates carved in stone or brick, bastions, protruding parts from the wall, and winding alleys. A fortress, that during the Middle Ages, could have been considered unconquerable.

Contrasting with the feeling of power, offered by these fortifications, the palaces, defended by them, and those inside some of the fortified towers, seem a weak, fragile and slim work of architecture. The archs of the doors of the fortress with stone and brick wedge-pieces comprise the frame structure of the fortress. The ones that decorate the court-yards and chambers of the *alcázares* are only ornamental. They do not support anything: apparently, they only rest on capitals of small columns, which seem to support them. Above these capitals rise wooden pilars up to the lintel, from which the lace-looking-plaster arch really hangs. In the same way, the stalactite-looking vaults that cover galleries and halls are supported by internal beams.

Gypsum, tiles and wood are the materials

4. —*Partial view of the Alhambra*

5.—*Mozarabic fragment, plaster decoration*

used in the decoration of the *Alhambra*. This decoration, though done with these poor materials, is indeed very beautiful. The small columns from the arcades, presenting a wide astragal and elegant cubic capital, along with certain tiles, constitute the only ornamental element in stone. They are light, slender and tall; the tiles, covering the socles and certain pavements, are rich and of great variety. The enameled ceramics reaches its highest peak and shows a remarkable polychromy; strangely beautiful, the stucco panels that cover the chamber walls. All the possible combinations with the geometric figures and floral drawings, that sometimes represent a symbolic expression of the inscriptions with which they mingle, are used; delicate and elegant is the wooden work that decorate the troughs and ceilings carved with knots and *tarácea*, showing materials such as ebony, ivory and nacre.

The sweet artistic impression of the *Alhambra* is specially caused by the magnificent gardens, which decorate its court-yards, and sorround the *alcázares* and palaces, scenting the atmosphere with myrtle and flower perfumes; the murmur of the water quietly running through the pools or noisily jumping in the fountains; the beautiful

comprehensive panorama of the palaces and fortresses; and the splendid and marvelous landscapes from the villages of *La Vega* and *Sierra Nevada* seen from its sighrseeing spots.

* * *

The *Alhambra* is on top of the northern hill, one of the two that form the *Cerro del Sol*, in whose slope is the *Generalife* situated. On the southern hill rise *Torres Bermejas*. The *Sabīka* Precipice, where, as said elsewhere, the forest lies today, separates both hills that are sorrounded by the *Rey Chico* slope, the *Darro* river and the lower houses of the city of Granada.

In ancient times both hills were inhabited, and there were fortifications at their summits. It seems that when the Arabs invaded this territory, there was a visigoth village on the hill, where the Alhambra is located today, and another jewish one at the base of *Torres Bermejas*. Rests of a ruined castle protected the former village, and the first fortifications of those towers defended the latter. These sites were the scenery of the battles between Arabs and Muladíes in the second half of the ninth century. According to the Arabian historians, the *qaysí* chief *Sawār ibn Hamdūn* rebuilt one of those castles. Since the works were done at night, at the light of torches, which gave the walls a red color, the Muladíes, the besiegers, gave it the name *al-hamrā'* meaning «the red».

Many years later, at the end of the eleventh century and the first third of the thiteenth century, during the African domination, those hills became once again the battlefield among Spanish Moslems, Almoravides and Almohades. The African's head-quarters were at the castle of *Albaycín*, built by the Ziries in the eleventh century, while the Spaniards had the old castle of *Torres Bermejas* as their principal fortress.

* * *

Muhammad al-Aymar, first Nasrite monarch of Granada, established his residence at the *alcazaba* of *Albaycín*. This had always been the government's quarters, and the only fortress

6.—*Dutch tile fragment* ▶

that could be defended, because the ones on the other hills were abandoned and ruined. Shortly after his proclamation, he decided to move his courship to one of these fortresses. In 1239, he went up to see them, studied them carefully, and chose the one that seemed to him the best one for his goals, and drew the sketches of the fortifications that were to be build. The chosen place was the same where the *Alcazaba* of the *Alhambra* stands today, which is separated by a precipice from the later palaces built, and from the *medina* or palatine city, which was constructed next to the *alcázares* protected from the winds.

Even though we do not have any historical or archaeological dats, it is possible that Muḥammad I himself ordered the building of the palaces. We know that the third monarch of the dynasty, also called Muḥammad, ordered the construction of the Mosque and the public baths of the palatine city; and it is possible that Ismācīl, the fifth sultan, would have sped up the works; but the most important builders of the Alhambra were Yūsuf I and his son Muḥammad V, who during their kingdom, built the two most important palaces of the place: the *Comares* and *Leones*.

* * *

Yūsuf I seems responsible for the building of the circumvallation wall that sorrounds and defends the palaces and *mediña*. When the wall approaches the fortifications of the *alcazaba*, it completely encloses the urban center of the *Alhambra*. This wall, except for its western side, which has disappeared, is almost completely preserved. It ran from the tower called of the Rocks, limit to the SE. of the fortresses of the *Alcazaba*, to Muḥammad's tower at the NE. of these fortresses. It reached the low stone wall of the *Alcazaba* by means of posterns.

Only one gate, called of the Wine, is preserved in the wall running from N. to S. Between this wall and the eastern part of the *Alcazaba* ran a steep street that ended at the entrance of the palaces, located at a lower level than that of the *medina* or palatine city, which had one of its entrances at the beginning of the street, right at the Gate of Wine. In 1494 the Christians built cisterns in the precipice, filled it with debris, leveled it and transformed it into a large and magnificent terrace, a splendid sightseeing place opened out upon the *Albaycín*. This zone has lately suffered a great transformation, due to the recent excavations done, that have unveiled the primitive street.

Twenty two powerful towers stand along the circumvallation wall. Most of them have an exclusive military purpose, being this the reason for their lack of ornaments. Others, however, without losing their military character, present sumptuous halls, exquisitely decorated, indicating that they once were the Prince's or rich men's quarters. The rampart from the first towers went inside them, where the military patrol would lodge; in the second ones, the ramparts divided the towers, thus forming independent rooms.

* * *

It seems that the entire site of the *Alhambra* had, during Moorish times, four principal entrances on the circumvallation wall and the *Alcazaba*: the Gate of Arms, called like this because those who wanted to go into the palace, had to leave their weapons there; this gate was located at the northwestern defenses of the *Alcazaba*; the Gates of *Explanada* and *Siete Suelos*, both built at the southern part of the wall, and the Gate of *Arrabal*, located at the northern zone of the wall, not far from the *Torre de los Picos*. To these four entrances, which still exist today, the Christians added one more, the *Puerta de los Carros*, which is also at the southern part of the wall, between the *Puerta de la Explanada* and *Siete Suelos*.

The gate, commonly known as *Judiciaria*, or of Justice and Law, but whose Arabic name, *šarīca*, must be interpreted as «esplanade», is the richest and the most magnificent of the four entrances to the *Alhambra* across the circumvallation wall, and together with the *Puerta de los Carros*, is today's usual entrance to the place. The powerful tower that defends it, is

10

10. *Esplanade Door, outlet*

named after this door, and stands on the lateral path at the left, which, beginning at the *Puerta de las Granadas*, runs across the forest By its inscription, we known that sultan Yūsuf I ordered to build it in 1348.

At the eastern wall of the tower, bordered by two protuding parts, there is a big pointed horseshoe arch presenting a brick panel and a lintel, where Fāṭima's hand, carved in marble, appears in its keystone. This arch leads to an open space and to an inner door, which also has a horseshoe arch carved in stone resting on small columns, and inscribed in a scotia and torus panel, with no other trimmings than shells on its keystone and spandrel. At the

central keystone of its lintel, there is a key, that together with the hand of the first arch, have a talismanic meaning. Hand and key are found on other doors of the *Alhambra*. Above the lintel, there is a band that carries the inscription of the origin; beautiful green, blue, and yellow Persian tiles of great archaeological value decorate the upper third of the portico, whose center is occupied by a niche that protects the Virgin and Child, sculptured at the beginning of the sixteenth century.

Following the second door, there is a hall with seats protected by archs which cover different types of vaults. Another arch, carved in bricks and magnificently decorated with tiles,

9. *Esplanade Door, also called Justice Door, entrance*

11. *Back view of the* Siete Suelos *Door*

gives way to the exit of the tower. The series of paintings, at the end of the alley, date from the end of the sixteenth century.

The *Puerta de Siete Suelos*, that the Moslems called *Bāb al Gūdur* or Gate of the Wells, maybe because of the many wells and dungeons nearby, is located at the tower of the same name, standing at the beginning of the avenue that leads to the *Generalife*. When Napoleon's troops left Granada in 1812, they blew up this and other towers of the circumvallation wall. Since then, tower and gate have stayed as ruins, until recently when they have been restored. A small tower or circular bastion defends them. This bastion, called of *Siete Suelos* because of the false belief that it had seven floors inside, really has two floors covered by cilindric vaults with skylights and loopholes in its walls.

The gate opens in a wall bordered by two fortified towers. Thanks to a drawing published by Murphy in 1813, we know that at the entrance of this tower, there was an elegant horseshoe arch, supported by small marble columns and decorated with geometric trimmings and shells on its *albanega*. On the central keystone appeared the talismanic key, which we have already mentioned. Above the lintel, there was a cursive script inscription with the Nasrite's emblem of the dynasty. Similar to *Puerta de la Explanada*, behind an inner arch, there was an alley with

14

a double arch at its exit. It was also, like the *Puerta de la Explanada,* one of the most remarkable gates of the *Alhambra.* Tradition gives the *Torre de los Siete Suelos* the responsability for the frightening tales that inspired Washington Irving to write one of his famous stories.

At the end of the slope that begins at the base of *Torre de los Picos,* an alley leads to the *Puerta del Arrabal.* It has a marked horseshoe arch built on *sillarejo* stone. Like the other gates from the circumvallation wall, the *Puerta del arrabal* also has the talismanic key in the keystone of its arch. The *Torre de los Picos* protects this door, which gives way to a bastion closed by another gate, which was built by the Christians and is known as the *Puerta del Hierro.*

The *Puerta de los Carros,* also built by the Christians in the circumvallation wall, lacks of any artistic or archaelogical interest. When we shall talk about the *Alcazaba,* we shall also refer to the *Puerta de las Armas.* It is commonly believed that this last gate was the entrance to the *Alhambra* for all those coming from the *Albaycín* environs, and from the eastern part of the *medina* of Granada. While the ones of *Explanada* and *Siete Suelos* were principally used by the inhabitants of the environs at the S. and W., of the *medina,* by the ones coming from the zones of *Alfareros* and *Loma,* and by those coming along the roads that led to *Guadix,* to the *Sierra Nevada*

12. — *The Alcazaba as seen from the Albaycín*

and to the *alquerías* or farms scattered on the southern part of the *Vega.* The *Puerta del Arrabal* could have been used as a link between the *Alhambra* and the palaces located at the base of the *Cerro del Sol,* especially Generalife.

* * *

It seems that the Nasrite's *alcazaba* has suffered very few transformations. Its construction began

13. *The Alcazaba as seen from Torres Bermejas (Red Towers)*

14. — *The Weapons Door*

in 1239 by Muḥammad ibn al-Aḥmar, the first sultan of the dynasty, and was ended around the middle of the thirteenth century. The principal modifications were done in the lower quarters of the fortress, which were transformed into a bastion for the artillery troops, and in part of the upper floor, which was modified at the end of the sixteenth century. A Cube, or small tower, was built next to the *Plaza de los*

15. — *Weapons Square*

Aljibes. It hid a tower and the *Puerta de la Tahona,* visible today, which connected the *alcazaba* with the royal palaces.

The fortress stands at the western and highest end of the residential zone of the *Alhambra.* This fortress presents a trapezoid shape some what irregular. The walls that sorround it are aproximately 1666 ft. long, 575 ft. at the longest part from E. to W., and 315 ft. at the widest zone. We do not know the names with which the Moors called the towers which are part of the *alcazaba.* Today we know them as *Torres de las Armas,* of *Alquiza, del Criado del Doctor Ortiz, del Homenaje, Quebrada, del Adarguero, de la Pólvora, de la Vela* and *de los Hidalgos.* There is another one, without name, at the southern part of the fortress, next to the Garden of *Adarves.*

Torre Quebrada, del Homenaje and *del Adarguero* rise at the E.; the ones of *la Pólvora, la Vela* and *los Hidalgos* at the W. To the N. stand *las Armas, del Criado del Doctor Ortiz* and *Alquiza,* and to the S. the one with no name next to the Garden of *Adarves.* From all of them, the ones of *la Vela, la Quebrada* and *del Homenaje* form the most powerful defenses of the fortress which is also protected by a wall. The archaeologists have observed in the *Alcazaba* foundations from buildings built before the thirteenth century. This suggests that Muḥammad al-Aḥmar used these ruins.

Coming today from the *Plaza de los Aljibes,* you go inside the *Alcazaba* through a modern entrance opened in the wall, and next to the *Torre del Adarguero,* which leads to the so called Garden of *Adarves;* it seems that the lower quarters had its entrance, during the Middle Ages, by a gate between the present wall and the one of the *Adarves.* The *Puerta de las Armas,* situated in the tower of the same name, gives way to the upper quarters. This gate, besides being an entrance to the *Alcazaba,* was also the only passageway for all those persons coming from *medina Garnata,* or bourgeois city, to *medīnat al-Ḥamrā'* or city of palaces.

This gate leads to the tower that defends it. The first horseshoe arch is carved in stone with brick strips protecting its spandrels and rests of tiles on its molding. After a quadrangular

16. — *Taper Tower* ▶

17. *Fountain in Adarves garden*

space, there is another brick arch that leads to several chambers covered by different types of vaults. Finally, another arch leads to the path that carries us to the *Puerta de la Tahona*. The *Puerta de las Armas* was connected with other fortifications of the *Alcazaba* by means of archs located to the right and left of the tower.

The space at the center of the fortress is considered as its parade ground. There are two cisterns and a silo. It was at this place where rests of some other chamber, probably a Moorish military room, were discovered. Next to this square, on the central street coming from the *Puerta de las Armas*, the garrison's bath, a very interesting piece of Archaeology, is located.

West of the parade ground stands the *Torre de la Vela*. It is the most famous tower of the fortress. Its imposing structure stands out above the city of Granada. Because of its great height, it was used as a watchtower of the *Vega*. Its bell still regulates the irrigation of this place. These characteristics have given birth to a song:

> *Quiero vivir en Granada*
> *porque me gusta el oír*
> *la campana de la Vela*
> *cuando me voy a dormir.*

You go inside this tower by a loophole opened on the second floor. It has four floors covered by several vaults. Cardenal Mendoza's cross was lifted on this tower and the Apostle James' and the royal flags were waved here on January 2, 1492, when the Christians took hold of the *Alhambra*. Every year, on the day before and on the Reconquest day, the bell of the *Vela* sounds until sunset. It is played by all those that want to do it, as a commemoration of that historical date. The same happens on the day of the Virgin of Rosary, when the victory of Lepanto is commemorated. From the plattform of the tower, we can see a magnificent view of the *Vega* of Granada. It recalls a carpet knitted with several shades of green, spotted by white villages and crossed by the *Genil* river which looks like a silver thread.

If the *Torre de la Vela* stands out above Granada, the *Torre del Homenaje*, the highest and most imposing of the place, does it above the *Darro* river valley and the *Albaycín* zone. It has five floors, three of which are divided into rooms (six in every floor) covered by vaults with semispheric and cilindrical edges. These chambers indicate that this tower was used for lodging. This tower, together with the *Vela* and *Torre Quebrada,* which has two floors, are the most powerful defenses of the fortified site.

Above the flat top of the southern part of the wall, the Marquis of Mondéjar built a garden at the beginning of the seventeenth century. He decorated it with fountains and beautiful columns, thus making one of the most romantic and pretty places of the *Alhambra*. From this site a marvelous view is seen to the special background. At the foreground, emerges the *Torre de la Explanada* among the trees of the Forest, which is limited, at one side, by the red sil-houette of *Torres Bermejas*, and to the other side by the Loma zone. The snow-capped peaks of Sierra Nevada make a beautiful background. To the right lies the city of Granada on the hill of *Mawrūr*, and reaches the *Vega*, sorrounded by bluish and grayish hills. Fortuny inmortalized the Garden of *Adarves* in his famous picture «*El jardín de los poetas*».

The same as in the *Alcazaba,* today you go inside the *Casa Real Vieja* of the *Alhambra* through a secondary entrance on the southern façade of the palace, traditionally known as *Mešwār;* during the Moslem occupation, the entrance to the *Casa Real* seems to have been located at the northern end of the street that ran along the base of the precipice, which divided the fortress from the palaces. You could either go along this street from the southern part of the place which had its entrance through the *Puerta de la Explanada,* or through the covered path that ran from the *Puerta de las Armas* to the *Puerta de la Tahona,* already described elsewhere. Only the ruins from the usual entrance to the palace, as well as to the *Mešwār,* are found today. They remained covered for many years with the debris used in the construction of the *Plaza de los Aljibes.* The excavations have revealed a small square which gives way to a yard sorrounded by galleries. On its southeastern corner there was a quadrangular-shaped building. A second yard, with a pool at its center, follows. The southern gallery of this courtyard has been preserved. It comprises nine archs with carved spandrels, resting on marble columns. This gallery to a tower decorated with *atauriques, mocárabes* and inscriptions; three small balconies open out upon this place, having the central one a beautiful carved wooden ceiling. The courtyard, gallery and tower are called of Machuca, because the architects Luis and Pedro Machuca lived there. According to the archaeologists, the tower, also called *Torre de los Puñales,* was built by sultan Yūsuf I.

The ruins from the palace of *Mešwār* have been so deeply transformed through the years, that it is difficult to know its primitive distribution. Bordering the eastern zone of Machuca's courtyard, there is an aisle that the Christians rebuilt, adding a new floor to the only one existing. It was first used to lodge the governors of the *Alhambra;* later Phillip V's Chapel was installed there. Its socle is decorated by Sevillan tiles, imitating the Arabian ones. Imperial eagles, Mendoza's shield and other

19. *Mešwār Room*

20

Castilian symbols mingle with the Nasrite's emblem.

A modern gate in the northern wall of this hall leads to a Moslem oratory, which had a previous entrance through an alley that connected it with Machuca's tower. It has suffered many restorations that do not enable us to recognize its primitive structure. On its eastern side, there is a *miḥrāb*, an open vaulted niche with a hroseshoe arch that covers a small eight-sided cupule. It is decorated with bows and inscriptions referring to sultan *Muḥammad* V who restored, or maybe built, the oratory.

In the eastern wall of the chamber, which was Phillip V's Chapel, already described, there is another door that leads to the courtyard of *Cuarto Dorado*, which is now arbitrarily called of the Mosque. A portico, formed by three archs supported by columns, appears at the northern façade. The two central marble columns are separated; the two lateral ones are covered by tiles and stand next to a wall. The first ones have strange capitals, that for some persons, resemble the zoomorphic type from Persepolis. At the portico, another arch, above which two smaller ones with jalousies appear, leads to the *Sala del Bosque,* a beautiful sightseeing place to the zone of the *Albaycín.* Wooden knots and tiles decorate the spandrels; on its carved wooden ceiling appear gothic paintings from the sixteenth century. This, together with the courtyard and the rest of the rooms of the *Mešwār,* have suffered many restorations and transformations.

The name *Mešwār* is given to this part of the palace, because it is believed that the chancery, the administration of the kingdom, the viziers' or ministers' offices, and the *kuttāb*'s or protocole secretaries' offices were installed here. It is very probable that the *Mešwār* could have been part of the palace of *Comares,* that some persons call *Serrallo.* At least it is so suggested by the latter's magnificent façade on the southern wall of the courtyard of *Cuarto Dorado.* This yard could have been the entrance to the *Patio de los Arrayanes* or to the *Patio de la Alberca,* which was the antechamber to the throne room,

also called of *Embajadores,* inside the *Torre de Comares.*

This beautiful and imposing façade, unique and precious work of Nasrite art, has two bodies. The first one has two linteled doors framed by beautiful tile works. Green, black, blue and honey brown tiles, on a white background, enclose stucco-decorated frames. A large panel, decorated with bows, separates both doors and their respective lintels with carved keystones in stucco. A beautiful tiled socle covers the lower part of the façade. On the second body, the two doors are substituted by two double mullioned window. Between these windows and the central panel of the first body, there is a small, stucco-framed window. The cornice presents a frieze, decorated with knots, formed by stalactite-looking archs supported by small columns. It is surmounted by another wooden frieze which presents an elegant inscription. A wide hood moulding, carved in wood and supported by long corbels, completes the decoration of this marvelous façade. Its stucco panels present geometric and floral drawings, shells, Nasrite's shields and inscriptions in cursive script and cufic lettering, some carrying a religious phrase, others praising sultan Muḥammad V.

It is well known that the palace of *Comares,* named after the tower where the throne room is, was built by sultan Yūsuf I. However, in some places, as in the façade just described, there are inscription referring to his son and successor, Muḥammad V; this is so, because the Nasrites used to replace quite often the decoration of the palaces built by the preceding sultans, even though the decoration did not need any restorations. Sometimes they placed stucco panels, decorated with inscriptions referring to them, over the existing decoration, without destroying it; ocassionally they completely changed the old ornamentation.

From the two gates in the southern façade of the courtyard of *Cuarto Dorado,* the one at the right connected this yard with the rooms at the *Mešwār.* The left one leads, along a winding alley, two the *Patio de los Arrayanes.* It is a marvelous antechamber of the throne

room and one of the places whose beauty has given the *Alhambra* its international fame. There is a beautiful pool, bordered by myrtles, on its center. The still waters are a mirror, where the magnificent porticos, north and south of the courtyard, are reflected, and where the silhouette of the *Torre de Comares,* where the throne room is, can be seen.

Years ago, a small fountain stood at the center of the pool; today the water is supplied by two modern faucets at each end of the pool. The clear blue water, the dark green myrtles, the whiteness of its pavement covered by white marbles tiles, the nacre from the arcades, and the red color of the tower make up a colorful picture, which the sun of Andalucía floods with light.

This yard and its rooms nearby are a perfect example of the Islamic-Granadine house: a rectangular yard with a pool at the center, porticos, at the end of the pool's longest axis, leading to suntously decorated galleries. These give way to luxuriant rooms, where the owner of the house entertained guests, and to lateral, cozy chambers, with no external decoration, where the family's private life was done.

Both porticos of the *Patio de los Arrayanes* face north and south. Each of them is formed by seven archs, being the central one the highest. This one rests on columns with stalactite-looking capitals and ornamented plasterwork spandrels showing a shell in the middle. The other six archs, supported by columns with cubic capitals, let the sunlight in through the trellised works in plaster that decorate them. The seven archs are framed with inscriptions, with cursive script the one that border the central arch, and cufic lettering around the rest of the archs.

The original ceiling of the northern gallery, as well as the one from the *Sala de la Barca,* were burned in 1890. They have been rebuilt, quite perfectly, with the pieces that could be saved from the fire and following previous drawings. The same thing happened to the small lateral fortified towers that stand in front of the big *Torre de Comares.* Previous to their restoration, there is proof of the existence of only one of them. A tiled socle covers the lower part of the gallery. This socle is not the original Arabian one, but an imitation done at the end of the sixteenth century. All along this socle there is an artistic inscription with cursive script and carved in plaster. It contains fragments from the poem written by Ibn Zamrak to Muhammad V in commemoration of the conquest of Algeciras. A wide stucco frieze, ornamented with geometric figures, pineapples and shells, completes the decoration of the gallery.

The southern portico comprises two bodies. The first one has a similar distribution to that of the northern portico. The second one has a gallery with six archs and a lintel. The door at the center of the portico led to rooms of the Arabian palace, partially located where Charles V's palace stands today, and which disappeared when the latter was built.

A beautiful pointed arch, at the center of the front part of the gallery, leads to the *Sala de la Barca,* antechamber of the throne room. This arch is decorated with stalactite-looking knots, and a beautiful floral design covers its spandrels. In its jambs, there are small niches or *tacas* presenting small archs bordered by inscriptions and geometric figures carved in marble. These *tacas* are lined with ceramics. At both sides of the walls, many other niches still have rests of the poetic inscriptions that decorated them.

The *Sala de la Barca* has its walls covered with works in stucco. Mingling with the Nasrite's symbol and the dynasty's code of arms, is the word *baraka,* or blessing, constantly repeated. The name of this room is probably a Spanish transcription of this word. This rectangular shaped hall, covered by a tiled socle, has at its ends two rooms with a tiled arch. An alley, inside the one at the right, leads to the *ḥammām* or royal bath.

One must walk below a double arch to go inside the *Salón de Embajadores,* or throne room. The first arch is at the center of the northern wall of the *Sala de la Barca;* the second one is in the wall that leads to the throne room. In the middle of both walls, there is a narrow

21. *Arrayanes courtyard with Southern side gallery*

22. *Arrayanes courtyard and Comares tower, seen drom the Southern side gallery*

alley with a small door at its right end, that leads to the upper quarters of the tower. The *mocárabes* in these archs still have patches of the previous paint; the one at the entrance presents three false jalousies, and the jambs from the one at the exit have *tacas*. Sorrounding these archs are inscriptions referring, like many others in the room, to sultan Yūsuf I.

The rectangular shape of the *Salón de Embajadores,* its height and marvelous decoration make it a perfect example of the Islamic-Granadine art. This room, one of the prettiest from the *Alhambra,* amazes the visitor. The marvelous ceiling, a masterpiece of Nasrite's wooden art, the stucco panels, covering the walls like singular tapestries, and the exquisite and different tiles that cover the socles, produce a deep impression on the visitor.

In each of the three external walls, there are three side rooms, located inside the wall which is almost 10 ft. wide. These rooms are used as *miradores,* or sight-seeing places. An arch leads the way to all of them. Their ceiling have a *mocárabe* ornamentation, their walls a rich stucco decoration, and their beautiful tiled socles are different in each of them, due to the different combinations and colors of the ceramic pieces.

It is almost sure that the thronc was located in the central side room in the northern wall. This is confirmed by a poem written on the stucco and by contemporary writers of the Reconquest. On top of the beautiful tiled socle, forming stars, rests a frieze of archs decorated with stalactite-looking *mocárabes.* The balcony of the central side room has two archs with small windows over its lintel. Similar to this one, though not so richly decorated, are the other two side rooms in the center of the eastern and western wall of the tower. They differ from the lateral ones in that these ones have only one arch that leads to the balcony. The first side room from the eastern wall was transformed into a gate when the corridor, that connects the tower with the Emperor's rooms, was built.

The ornamented plaster works, which cover the walls of the halls from the socle up to the cornice, are a magnificent example of decorative art in gypsum. The decoration is based on the combination of geometric figures, principally rhombus, large rosettes and stars, slender vegetables figures and elegant cursive and cufic letters of the Arabian alphabet.

The dome carries three cedar-wood panels formed by millions of small pieces, many of them still having their original paint. A similar panel, having a big tower decorated with *mocárabes* at its center, crowns the dome. It all represents the artistic expression of the seven skies eschatologic concept of the Moslem's paradise. Geometric drawings combined with million of stars make a remarkable masterpiece.

The circumvallation wall links the *Torre de Comares* with the one called *Abū-l-Ḥaŷŷāŷ.* It rises from the walk behind the parapet of the wall, and the entrance to its upper floor, known as *Tocador de la Reina,* is located in the side room, at the *Salón de Embajadores.* This side room was transformed into a gate, and it also connects the above hall with the Emperor's rooms. The *Tocador de la Reina* was added by the Christians in the middle of the sixteenth century. The walls of this part of the tower are decorated with valuable historical paintings, representing Charles V's expedition to Tunez. The Garden of *Lindaraja* leads to the lower floor of the tower across a door with a wooden lintel decorated with inscriptions. Above the door, fragments of the poem written to celebrate Muḥammad V's return to the kingdom of Granada can be seen carved in plaster. Inscriptions, referring to sultan Yūsuf I, appear in the room of the tower; among the worn off ornamental elements, the socle painted on stucco and the tiles with beautiful floral, deer and even human beings paintings, offer a special interest.

The *hammām* or royal bath is similar to the Roman hot baths. It has three halls. The first one, commonly known as *Camas,* corresponds to the classic apodyterium and presents two floors. The upper one rests on the walls and on four columns, leaving an open space where a fountain stands at the center. The hall is sorrounded by narrow galleries in both floors. Two of its walls present *alhanías* or beds covered

23. *Arrayanes courtyard, northern side gallery*

with tiles, which are reached by twin archs. The hall was named after these beds. Its walls are covered by colorful ceramic and stucco trimmings; except for the columns and some tiles, all its decoration corresponds to years after the Arabian domain, when it was deeply renewed. The upper floor is almost at the same level than the *Sala de la Barca,* from where a narrow alley at its right end connects it with the *ḥammam,* as it was said before.

Segmented archs lead to the tepidarium and caldarium. The tepidarium is bordered by porticos with horseshoe archs. The caldarium is divided into three rooms, separated too by horseshoe archs. These two chambers are paved with marble slabs covered by tiled socles. At the right and left of this hall, there are two basins, having the last one a niche with a poetic inscription carved in marble.

* * *

The palace of *Comares,* built by Yūsuf I, had a double function: it was the courtship's living place as well as the sultan's private quarters. It has already been said that Yūsuf I's son, Muḥammad V, made important restorations in the palace. He changed the decoration of

28

24. *Entrance to the Barca Room* ▶

27. *Upper part of the Beds' Room*

some of the rooms and decorated others that lacked ornamentation. This monarch added to the palace of *Comares*, a new one called *de los Leones*, which sheltered the king's and his relatives' private life. He built it next to the old palace, but independently from it. Its different and uneven plattforms, being the lowest a garden, resemble the *cármenes* of Granada or villas.

The wall that closes the eastern part of the *Patio de los Arrayanes*, the bath from the palace of *Comares* and the circumvallation wall with the tower of *Abū-l-Ḥayŷāŷ* at its center, are the limits to the West and North of the palace of *Leones*. It is limited to the E. and S. by streets and houses from the palatine city of the *Alhambra*. When the Christians built the Emperor's rooms next to the flat top of the wall, the garden

28. – *Hammām or Bathroom of the Comares palace*

was changed into what we know today as *Patio de Lindaraja*. The *Patio de los Leones*, with the beautiful fountain which gives this place its name, is built on the central plattform, sorrounded by the most important rooms of the palace. It was possible the existence of a garden around the fountain; it was also probable that the slender columns and the small lace-looking archs were to represent the palms of an oasis.

The highest plattform was the king's favourites chambers, according to the historian Ibn al-Jatīb. Part of these rooms was destroyed when Charles V's palace was built. The only things that remain today are a small courtyard and two galleries sorrounding it. From the original porticos, only the western one still remains. It is formed by three archs with ornamented spandrels. From the columns that supported them, only the two of the center are to be found today. Their black capitals carved in marble look like an eleventh century work, previous to the Nasrite's art. It undoubtedlycomes a monument, now non-existent. At the center of the portico of the gallery, an arch, bordered by stucco inscriptions, led to a small hall. The walls from the gallery around the courtyard are covered by an interesting socle which is not tiled, but painted on plaster with bright red, black and blue colors. This room of the palace is partially on top of the *Sala de los Abencerrajes* and of a pool next to it. Its present entrance is located at the western end of the gallery, that leads to a small staircase.

It has been pointed out, that the *Patio de los Leones* is the central axis of the palace. It is named after the twelve carved lions that support the fountain at the center of the courtyard. It is a moorish sculpture though of doubtful origin. Lately, it has been attributed to a Hebrew artist of the eleventh century. The rectangular courtyard is framed by a gallery, whose portico present single, double or groups of three or four slender, Macael white, marble columns. Their cubic decorated capitals present, on their abacus, praising inscriptions referring to Muhammad V. These columns link stucco trellised archs, through which the sunlight filters. The

decoration is based on inscriptions and geometric figures. A carved wooden socle supports the hood moulding.

From the center of the eastern and western galleries, two side rooms sorround the fountain. They have a quadrangular shape with a wooden dome which rests on a frieze ornamented with *mocárabes*. The galleries and side rooms from the *Patio de los Leones*, like the rest of the rooms of the palaces and even some of the towers, had tiled roofs. The tiled socle, that decorated the walls of the galleries, has disappeared, and the wooden hood mouldings have been successively restored. According to Christians writers that visited it just after the Reconquest, the galleries were paved with white marble slabs, as they are today.

Ibn Zamrak, poet of the *Alhambra*, was very lucky because his poems were carved in stucco or sculpted in marble, being this an important characteristic of the decoration of the palace. One of poems is carved on the edge of the dodecagonal cup which rests on the twelve lions that form the fountain. In his poems, praising sultan Muhammad V, he beautifully describes the running water of the fountain.

The shape of the *Patio de los Leones* does not closely follow the characteristics of the Nasrite house, which usually have two porticos at both ends of the longest axis of the central pool. The archaeologists find some similarity between this courtyard and Monteagudo's palace, built in the twelfth century, completely destroyed today. The courtyard from *al-Qarawiyyīn de Fez* mosque is an obvious copy of the *Patio de los Leones*. It is our courtyard where the Nasrite art reaches its maximum beauty and splendor.

The gallery gives way to four large halls bordering the courtyard. One of them, called *Dos Hermanas*, has other smaller rooms next to it. Artists and archaeologists agree when they consider that all the esthetic factors, which make the *Alhambra* one of the prettiest monuments of the world, are compiled in this hall. Its structural elements are perfectly and harmoniously distributed, because rooms and walls alternate symmetrically but in a diversity of ways; the rooms follow each other in a way

35

that gives an amazing perspective with a beautiful view as the background. Its decoration, the richest, prettiest and most elegant of the *Alhambra*, has its maximum splendor in the magnificent cupula. Ibn Zamrak, in his passionate poems, described it as «even more beautiful than the marvelous dome of heaven.»

A double arch, separated by a narrow alley, leads to the quadrangular hall. These archs present *mocárabes* in their concave faces and stucco trimings in their spandrels. Another similar arch, opened in the opposite wall, leads to the *Sala de los Ajimeces*, antechamber of the *Mirador de Daraja*. In the middle of each of the two left rooms, two archs, similar to the ones described, give way to several small halls with less important dependencies or *alhanías*. Above these archs, four small windows, from the upper rooms, open out to the entrance hall.

The socle, which covers its walls, is a masterpiece of Granada's tile industry. It is built with metal-glazed tiles forming colorful strips shaped as poligons with the Nasrite motto, «wa-là gālib illá Allāh» in golden letters at their centers. This socle also amazes for its extraordinary and exquisite richness. There is a stucco band, above this socle, where part of Ibn Zamrak's poem is carved, describing the room and its dome. Panels of hewn plaster follow, with stars and fringes with inscriptions in cufic and cursive scripts decorating it.

Squinches, hewn with bows and ending in slender small columns, are located at the four corners of the hall above the small windows from the upper floor. They change the shape of the courtyard from a square into an eight-sided figure on which the dome rests. New bands with inscriptions and stucco trimmings appear. In each side of the octagonal figure, there are two small windows responsible for the gentle illumination of the dome. It is formed by eight sided bands which get narrower every time, until they enclose the concave pyramid, which they themselves build, into a star. The unequal beauty and structure of this dome causes the admiration of all the visitors.

The *Sala de las Dos Hermanas*, named after

two big marble slabs which constitute its pavement or, according to others, after the legend of two captive sisters who died from love, gives way through an arch, opened in its northern wall, to the *Sala de los Ajimeces*. This is named after the archs leading to the Garden of *Lindaraja*. It has a rectangular shape, covered by a vault of *mocárabe* which is not the original one. Part of its walls presents stucco trimmings and inscriptions.

To the *Mirador de Lindaraja* you go through a big arch in the center of the wall where arches windows are. This big arch presents a wide concave face with stalactite-looking bows and stucco trimmings on its spandrels. Its jambs have *tacas* and beneath them appears a beautiful tiled socle formed by tiny pieces. This socle comprises a black-tiled strip with a praising poem to Muḥammad V and a description of the chamber. Underneath, there is a panel with geometric drawings, where poligons and stars intermingle.

Three small windows are opened to the *miradores*. The central one is the widest and presents twin linteled archs, which support themselves on small columns with square capitals. The central column stands alone, while the other two are next to the wall. The small windows from the lateral walls have only one arch, similar to the one described. The three windows are inside an arcade with its concave face decorated with *mocárabes*. Except for the tiled socle whose decoration is not as rich as the jambs of the entrance arch, the entire chamber presents a magnificent stucco decoration with geometric figures and large bands with inscriptions. The pavement still has rests of its primitive ceramics. The roof is formed by a hewn wooden ceiling with stained glasses. The window sills are extremely low so that the persons, sitting on their knees as the moorish costume asks for, could see the delicious view of the garden, the *Darro* valley and the zone of *Albaycín*. This was so until the Emperor's chambers were built, hiding that wonderful view.

In passing the southern part of the gallery of the *Patio de los Leones*, one goes into the *Sala*

de los Abencerrajes. Tradition tells that this hall is named after the bloody historical event in which the principal knights from Granada's clan of *Abencerrajes* were murdered here; it is said that the stain of iron oxide which darkens the basin is due to the blood shed by the knights.

A double arch, separated by a narrow alley, leads to this chamber, in a similar way as in the entrance to *Dos Hermanas*. The *Sala de los Abencerrajes* has a quadrangular shape, is paved with white marble slabs and is covered by a beautiful and elegant dome, whose walls are decorated with stucco. It was partially rebuilt in the sixteenth century, when the Arabian

33.—*Fountain of the Lions*

34.—*Detail of the Fountain of the Lions* ▶

36. *Cupola or dome of Two Sisters Room*

tiles were substituted by the present Christian ones. Double archs, in the eastern and western walls of the chamber, supported by columns with magnificent carved capitals, lead to chambers or *alhanías* covered by a ceiling decorated with painting of the sixteenth century.

The alley, which separates the arch at the entrance of the chamber, has small doors to the right and left. From the left one, a stircase leads to the upper dependencies, which are distributed around the Harem courtyard, already described. The alley reaches the fortified tower which has been considered for a long time as a Nasrite *rawḍa* or graveyard. Perhaps at the end of that alley, there was an entrance to the palace of the *Leones*; but it seems that its principal entrance must have been on the opposite end of the alley. This one runs parallel to the southern gallery of the courtyard, to a rectangular room divided into two compartments. In the western façade of this room, which faced toward a narrow street, that has disappeared, was probably located the most noble gate from the palace. The cistern, which supplied the water for the palace, was located between the *Sala de los Abencerrajes* and the room which has been described before.

Today you go inside the *Patio de los Leones* through the lower rooms of the eastern part of the *Patio de los Arrayanes.* This zone, opened

45

after the Reconquest, leads us to the *Sala de los Mocárabes*, which closes, to the West, the first of the described courtyards. This chamber is named after the decoration of the dome which is only partially preserved today. From an artistic point of view, it is the least important from the four rooms around the courtyard. Its walls are decorated with stucco, and in its western wall, three archs lead to the gallery.

The *Sala de los Reyes*, the biggest of the palace, is located behind the eastern gallery of the courtyard. It occupies a large rectangle, and you go inside by passing three beautiful proticos, each having triple archs decorated with bows and supported by slender columns. It is divided into five compartments. The three central ones, that constitute the entrance, are quadrangular shaped. The sides present rooms at their ends, thus the room is really divided into five departments. These are separated by pointed double archs with their concave face decorated with stalactite-looking *mocárabe* and stucco works in their spandrels. There are stucco strips around them, with inscriptions praising Muḥammad V. The departments rest on columns covered with tiles.

Domes, of *mocárabe* style, cover the five compartments. Each of them has at its rear end a small side room. Besides its suntuous decoration and its distribution, that produces a beautiful perspective, one must admire the paintings on each of the ceilings of the side rooms. The central painting, done on leather, represents ten probable Moslems monarchs (after which the room was named as *Sala de los Reyes*) talking and sitting on pillows. The ones from the lateral side rooms represent chivalrous scenes. There is a strong discussion about the author or authors of these paintings. Some consider them done by Moslem artists, others by Christians, and still others by paintors of the Italian school.

* * *

Before leaving the Arabian Palaces, we must refer briefly to the important modifications done by the Christians. It seems that the palaces were sorrounded by gardens located in the space

38. –*Abencerrajes Room*

between the circumvallation wall and the walls of the two fortresses. This was so from *Torres de Comares*, described elsewhere, to *Abū-l-Ḥayyāy* tower, and from here to the *Torre de las Damas*, which will be described later. During the first third of the sixteenth century, the corridors and chambers from *Torre de Comares* to the *Abū-l-Ḥayyāy*, were built. These chambers are known as the Emperor's rooms, because they were used by Charles V and his courtship.

The garden, at the North of the Palace of the *Leones*, was then sorrounded by walls. This garden began at the base of the *Sala de las Dos Hermanas's* sightseeing place, in the lowest plattform which was transformed into the delicious and romantic courtyard of *Patio de Lindaraja*; between the flat top of the wall and the *Patio de Comares* appeared another melancholic courtyard,

Reja, also called of the Cypresses, because of the four centanary trees around its modern fountain.

To the Emperor's room one goes in through the first side room in the western wall from the *Salón de Embajadores,* as it has been described. This side room, later transformed into gate, leads through a corridor to a huge hall, maybe the antechamber to the Emperor's room. Four doors arc present in this chamber. The one at the West is the entrance gate; the northern one leads to the *Peinador de la Reina* on top of the tower of *Abū-l-Haŷŷāŷ;* the one at the east connects the chamber with four rooms built on top of the gallery that closes the northern part of the *Patio de Lindaraja.* These four rooms are called Washington Irving chambers because it was here where he lived when he wrote his famous *Cuentos de la Alhambra;* finally, the one at the South leads to the *Cuadra del Artesón de Madera,* located above the western gallery of the *Patio de Lindaraja,* which is next to the upper floor of the Comares bath. The *Cuadra del Artesón* links with the western chamber of the *Sala de las Dos Hermanas.* The most interesting characteristic of the Emperor's chamber is its rich ceilings decorated with carved panels.

The chambers next to the southern portico of the *Patio de los Arrayanes* were destroyed in order to build Charles V's Palace. Pedro Machuca designed the palace and started its building, which was followed by his son Luis and other architects. They sttained one of the most perfect Spanish Renaissance masterpieces. Its massive building elements and its sober ornamentation contrast with the delicate and exquisite architecture of the neighboring Nasrite palaces or *alcázares.*

This quadrangular palace, formed by two bodies, has a large courtyard in its center, sorrounded by galleries. In the first body, a dome sorrounds the courtyard. This cupola is supported by single Doric columns which correspond to pillars next to the inner wall. Niches are present between the pillars. The palace

42. – *Bas-relief on the Charles V Palace*

was not completely built. From the upper floor, only the Ionian columns could be built. Only recently have they been covered with a fairly good ceiling.

The Italian chimney room is the most outstanding from all the chambers around the courtyard. Only three, from the four façades of the palace, are decorated. The northern façade lacks decoration because it is a common wall to this palace and the *Comares* palace. The most outstanding from the other three, is the western one which has a magnificent gate at its center. Three doors lead to the first body. They are separated by four double Doric columns, that rest on bases with beautiful bas-reliefs. In the second body, instead of doors, there are three large windows with medallions on top. José Zorrilla, king of the Spanish poets,

was crowned at Charles V's palace. The courtyard is changed into an unequal auditorium during the International Festival of Music.

* * *

As it was said, some of the towers have suntuous palaces inside, which were once the Nasrite princes' and rich men's quarters. The most important of all is the one at the *Torre de las Damas*, located on the Gardens of *Partal*. Maybe its name was given because of the magnificent portico that limits these gardens to the North. These gardens, recently renewed, are limited by the *Patio de Lindaraja*, the façade from the *Sala de los Reyes* and Charles V's Palace. The southern part of the gardens presents uneven

43. — *Partial view of Charles V
Palace courtyard* ▶

44.—*Ladies' pond
and tower*

45. — *Lions of the maristān decorating the pond of the Ladies' tower*

plattforms that continue in a large terrace up to the circumvallation wall where the *Torre de las Damas* rises. At the East from these gardens, well preserved ruins of other palaces can be found today.

The palace, *Torre de las Damas*, have suffered great alterations. Only the portico with its gallery, a small quadrangular room, a sightseeing place on the upper floor and a beautiful pool in front of the portico stand today. The façade comprises five archs from which, only the central one preserves its *mocárabe* decoration. These archs rested on columns. When the tower was restored, they rested on brick pillars, which have recently been substituted by small columns, resembling the original ones. The ceiling of the gallery presents a decoration in *mocárabe* with a dome at its center. A big arch in the front part of the portico leads to a hall. The decoration of the arch comprises beautiful flower ornaments on its spandrels and suntuous niches in its concabe face. Nine small balconies offer us a delicious view from the *Albaycín* and *Darro* valley. The socle and walls show rests of the original tiles and stucco trimmings. Inscriptions in cufic letters with fragments of poems and praising phrases complete the decoration. It has been considered as the most exquisite and delicate ornamentation of the palaces of the *Alhambra*.

The two lions, at the end of the pool, opposite to the portico, were brought from the *maristán* or hospital, which was built by sultan Muḥammad V at Ajsāris. To the left of the tower, a small house presents paintings of human beings, considered of great archaeological value. To the right of the tower, a small Moslem praying place has suffered many restorations. The *Torre de los Picos* and *Cadi*, rising on top of the circumvallation wall, following the *Torre de las Damas*, have no great interest from an artistic point of view, since they were built only for military purposes.

It does not happen the same thing with the *Cautiva* palace, one of the most beautiful palaces of the place. It has three floors: low, principal and high. You go into the principal floor through a winding alley which ends in a courtyard. This has four horseshoe archs resting on stucco-covered pillars. At the courtyard's rear end, there is a double arch with knots in its concave face and *tacas* in its jambs. Over it appear three small windows closed by jalousies. This arch gives way to a square room. The rest of the walls present side rooms with archs supported by half columns. The side rooms are apened to the exterior by a window with two archs separated by a slender marble column with a cubic capital. The socle is covered with beautiful tiles, and the walls by rich stucco trimmings. Cursive and cufic inscriptions in stucco and tiles are the principal decoration of the chamber. Some inscriptions contain poetic descriptions of the tower, others, religious phrase and praises to sultan Yūsuf I, its buildre. Neither its ceiling, nor its pavement are the original ones.

The inscriptions, decorating the chambers of the *Torre de las Infantas*, refer to sultan Sacd, Boabdil's grand-father. Boabdil was the last Nasrite Monarch of Granada, so the decoration of these chambers should have been done, at least, in the middle of the fifteenth century. Consequently it is one of the last masterpieces of the Spanish-Moslem art. Besides, this fact is confirmed by the lower quality of its decoration, compared to those from the other palaces. You go inside this Tower through a yard. At its left, a staircase goes up to the upper floor; to the right, another staircase leads to the terrace. A horseshoe arch with *tacas* in its concave face, gives way to the central hall, which has two galleries. The modern ceiling replaced the primitive stalactite-looking one. The poets have idealized the *Torre de la Cautiva* and the *Infantas*. In the latter, Washington Irving's stories, *Zayda*, *Zoraida* and *Zorahaida*, took place.

Rests of another Arabian palace are found at San Francisco's Convent, the Catholic Queen's first tomb. Today it has been transformed into *Parador Nacional de Turismo* (a hotel financed by the government). All along the zone known as *secano*, ovens, baths, tanneries from the ancient palatine city of the *Alhambra*, are found.

* * *

46.—*Captive tower*

47.—*Room in the Captive tower*

49. — *The Spanish National Orchestre interprets in Charles V Palace Mahler's 8th Symphony during the International Music Festival*

During Spring and Summer, the *Alhambra* and its Forest make a magnificent scenery where a religious and prophane event take place respectively. The image of the *Virgen de las Angustias*, kept at *Santa María* church, is taken out on a procession through the lighted forest, every Holy Week thursday at sunset. Her appearance through the *Puerta de la Explanada,* among the lights and the public's acclamation, gives a striking and impressive feeling.

During the last days in June and the first ten days of July, the International Festival of Music and Dance is held in the *Alhambra* and the *Generalife:* symphonic concerts at Charles V's Palace, singers at the courtyards of *Arrayanes* and *Leones,* and *ballet* at the *Generalife* gardens. It is not only the exceptional quality of the performers, but the unique and magnificent scenery where these events take place, that attracts people from all parts of the world.

48. – *Procession of Ste. María de la Alhambra*